D0718926

ARE YOU really A GENIUS?

Timeless Tests for the Irritatingly Intelligent

Robert A. Streeter & Robert G. Hoehn

Bodleian Library
UNIVERSITY OF OXFORD

This edition first published in 2015 by the Bodleian Library
Broad Street
Oxford OX1 3BG

www.bodleianshop.co.uk

ISBN: 978 1 85124 423 2

First published as *Are You a Genius?* by Robert A. Streeter and Robert G.
Hoehn, Newnes, London 1935.

Designed and typeset by Dot Little at the Bodleian Library in 9 on 11
Georgia
Printed and bound on 90gsm munken cream by TJ International Ltd.,
Padstow, Cornwall

British Library Catalogue in Publishing Data
A CIP record of this publication is available from the British Library

CONTENTS

ANSWERS

PREFACE

A FAMOUS statesman once said, 'What this country needs is good beer at twopence a pint.' We really disagree. We feel that perhaps a few more Geniuses might prove to be the salvation. So we have set about to create some. Incidentally this little book provides entertainment of a sort that has been popular throughout the ages in that it matches wits. Most of the questions are psychological in type—they require a mind that resembles an active mountain goat rather than a saturated sponge. In other words they necessitate agility of mind rather than book learning.

A few of the questions will be recognized as old favourites which probably caused nervous disorders several generations ago. To the unknown, deceased geniuses who originated them we extend thanks and sing praises after having feebly attempted to emulate their ability in creating mental confusion and psychic chaos among men.

We must also acknowledge with profuse appreciation the assistance and patience of the faculty and students of the Kingsley School, who have martyred themselves by acting as our experimental victims. They have lived, much like the superstitious man who walks in a cemetery at midnight, in fearsome apprehensive terror of being suddenly jumped out upon by an ogre—in the form of one of the authors with an evil smile and a catch question. Their few errors can be interpreted only as verification of the statement of Francis Bacon: 'A sudden, bold, and unexpected question doth many times surprise a man and lay him open.'

THE AUTHORS, 1935

HOW TO FIND A GENIUS

Scoring

Sneak up on your friends and spring the questions on the following pages. For all except the last question in each group, score the one who answers first correctly one point. The final question in each group is a 'brain-twister' and is worth three points. High score discloses the Genius.

If you have no friends, try the test by yourself, recording your time. In this case each of the first nine questions counts ten. The last one counts thirty. If you equal or better the score and time made by the notable whose name and grade appear before the test, you may be very certain that you are a Genius. If you find that you are not a Genius, don't be discouraged—remember 'It's only a step from Genius to Insanity.'

For an explanation of scoring, see page 7

TEST 1

Possible Score 120

1   Rearrange the following letters so as to make the name of a living creature:

    B R I N O

2   Four men can build 4 boats in 4 days. How long will it take one man to build one boat?

3   Test your memory on this passage:

Three men and their wives and a widower left by automobile at noon one day for a picnic. After they had gone 3 miles, they saw two men and a child in a car that had broken down. 'That is tough luck', said one of the picnickers. At one o'clock they arrived at the picnic grounds, where they saw only the old one-armed caretaker and his son. They immediately started to eat their luncheon of sandwiches, fruit and cake.

Question: How many people have been mentioned?

4   The hands of a clock indicate that the time is 1.20. If the hour hand were where the minute hand is and vice versa, what time (to the nearest five minutes) would it be?

5   Which is heavier, milk or cream?

6   A man starts from a given point. If each time that he takes two steps forward he must take one backwards, how many steps will he have to take in order to reach a point five steps ahead of his starting point?

7   What one word means both 'dodge' and 'immerse'?

8   Excluding pennies, how many different combinations of coins will make half a crown.

9   What is the fallacy in the following interesting story told by an aviator?

During the war I watched a friend of mine who was flying alone on an observation flight above the lines. When he had completed his mission and was on his way home, thinking to himself how lucky he was not to have seen an enemy plane, an Austrian aviator suddenly swooped upon him from above a cloud bank, and shot him to the ground. He was dead when the first person reached him.

'Brain Twister'

10　A fruit-vendor had a basket of oranges. A customer approached him and purchased one-half of the oranges plus one-half of an orange. A second customer came and bought one-half of what he had left plus one-half an orange. A third customer purchased one-half of what was then left plus half an orange. After this sale the vendor had no oranges. He had not cut or broken an orange. How many did he have when he started?

TEST 2

Possible Score 100

1   A. can dig a ditch in 3 days. B. can dig the same ditch in 6 days. How long will it take them working together to dig it?

2   What fraction (within one-tenth) of a piece of floating ice is under water?

3   If 6 and 3 are 9, answer 'wrong' unless 6 and 3 are not 8, in which case answer 'right'.

4   If the eleventh day of the month falls on Tuesday, what day of the week will the 30th be?

5   What is the largest number that can be made by rearranging the digits in the number

38,017?

6   What is the fallacy in the following story?

Mr. Drake was driving his car along a straight highway which led to his destination, a town in Florida, about 20 miles north of his starting-point. When he had gone approximately 19 miles, a fast-moving car passed his. As a result his car was forced a couple of yards off the highway, thereby scraping its side against some protruding bushes. He stopped his car, and, as he was looking out of the window to ascertain whether any noticeable damage had been done by the bushes, he judged from the position of the sun that it was late in the afternoon and that he would have to hurry. A couple of minutes later he arrived at his destination, happy in the thought that he had escaped a possible serious accident.

7 A boy buys a bat and a ball for 1s. 6d. If the bat costs him a shilling more than the ball, how much does he pay for the ball?

'Brain Twister'

8 Rearrange the letters in the word 'sleuth' to make another word.

TEST 3

Possible Score 120

1   What word meaning 'ship' would mean 'small collections of water' if the letters were read back wards?

2   How many different three-digit numbers can be made from the digits 1, 2, and 3?

3   In the year 1938, the first day of February falls on Monday. What day of the week does the last day of February fall on?

4   Which is the greatest distance?

    10 FT   3½ YDS   124 INCHES

5   An inaccurate historian wrote the following account:

The early American colonists were a liberty-loving people. Because of the conditions imposed upon them they held numerous public meetings to determine what course of action to pursue. At one of these gatherings Thomas Jefferson sounded the keynote of their attitude when, in a memorable speech, he said, 'Give me liberty or give me death.' Benjamin Franklin, who officially represented the colonies in England and France, was another loyal colonist. While in England in 1775, just previous to the revolution, he wisely advised Englishmen against the policy then being employed by Charles II and his ministry. Satisfaction was not given to the colonists, however, and finally by the signing of the Declaration of Independence in New York, on July 4, 1776, these men signified definitely their determination to enjoy liberty.

Question: What three errors in historical fact has the historian made?

6   It takes normally 30 minutes to fill a tank. If, however, a hole allows one-third of the water being poured in to escape, how long will it take to fill the tank?

7   B is to E as 2 is to what number?

8   If the word POD were printed in small letters, how would it read if viewed upside down?

9   The records of Scotland Yard state the following facts in relation to the gruesome murder of Mr. Adolphus Crane. Remember as much of the account as possible:

The sergeant at the desk of a police station received the alarm in the form of a telephone message from Mr. Crane's butler, Whitney, at 2.10 in the morning. Whitney pleaded for speedy assistance, saying that he knew definitely who the murderer was. Detectives McCarthy and Blair were immediately dispatched to the house. They arrived at three o'clock. At 3.05 the sergeant received another call, which proved to be the detectives. They had discovered that Whitney had been murdered also. Killed by a shot through the head, he lay in a pool of his own blood. Mr. Crane's death had been caused by a severe beating on the head with a blunt object. The mystery was never unravelled. No clues were discovered. The murderer had effectually destroyed the only avenue of approach by killing poor Whitney.

Question: Between what specific times must Whitney have been murdered?

'Brain Twister'

10 A man having a 7-gallon measure and a 4 gallon measure and no other container of any description goes to a well to get exactly 5 gallons of water. How does he do it?

TEST 4

Possible Score 120

1   A man lived in a house that could be entered by only one door and five windows. Making certain that there was no one in the house one day, he went out for the afternoon. Upon his return, although the windows were still locked and unbroken and the door had not been forced, he discovered a thief in his house robbing it. If the thief did not use a skeleton key, or pick any of the locks, how did he get into the house?

2   If a clock is stopped for a minute every 10 minutes, how long will it take the minute hand to complete a revolution?

3   Within an inch, what is the distance around the base of an ordinary pint milk bottle?

4   A father is three times as old as his son. In ten years he will be twice as old. How old is the father at present?

5   What two 4-letter words pronounced the same but spelled differently mean 'valley' and 'curtain'?

6   If 1 = a, 2 = b, 3 = c, etc., what word of five letters
    does the following number make?

    $$3\,8\,,9\,4\,5$$

7   If viewed upside down, what number would the
    following digits make?

    $$6\,1\,9\,6\,1$$

8   A is 5 inches taller than B.

    C is 5 inches shorter than A.

    What is C's height in relation to B's?

9   Listen carefully to the following extracts from the
    diary of Robinson Crusoe:

    *August 17. Spent the day chiefly in gathering my
    plentiful harvest of barley. Found that my pit had
    entrapped for me a female goat and her kid.*

    *August 18. Due to rain I worked most of this day on
    perfecting my grindstone and arranging my tools.*

    *August 19. Because of continued wet weather, I
    worked on the tasks of the previous day and found
    that my new grindstone was quite serviceable.*

    *August 20. The weather was very hot. I devised a
    sort of umbrella to give me shade. I made it from
    the skin of the she-goat, which I had killed, the idea
    coming to me because of the discomfort caused by
    the sun beating on me all day.*

August 21. On this day after a shower in the morning I explored the island, taking as my equipment my parasol, a hatchet, and a saw.

Question: On how many days did it rain?

'Brain Twister'

10 Two volumes of a thousand pages each are arranged properly in a bookcase. Each volume is 2 inches thick, including the covers, each of which is one-eighth of an inch thick. If a bookworm eats his way from page 1, volume 1, to page 1000, volume 2, what distance does he travel?

TEST 5

Possible Score 120

1   Does one 2-inch pipe fill a tank of water at the same speed, less quickly, or more quickly than two 1-inch pipes?

2   What adjective which means 'pertaining to citizenship' spells the same from right to left as it does from left to right?

3   Mr. Smith, while out walking one day, recognized a boyhood friend whom he had not seen nor heard about for more than ten years. His friend, after greeting Mr. Smith warmly, said, 'I suppose that you do not know that I am married to some one whom I met shortly after I lost track of you. Here comes my daughter now.'

'How do you do?' said Mr. Smith, addressing the little girl. 'What is your name?'

'I am named after my mother', replied the child.

'Oh, so your name is Catherine too?' said Mr. Smith.

'Yes', answered the girl, 'but how did you know?'

How did Mr. Smith know that the girl's name was Catherine?

4   A Yorkshireman married a widow, and they each already had children. Ten years later there was a pitched battle in which the present family of twelve children were violently engaged. The mother came running to the father crying: 'Come at once! Your children and my children are fighting our children!' As the parents now had each nine children of their own, how many were born during those ten years?

5   Name a Prime Minister of the last forty years whose surname begins with 'R'.

6   What number expressed in Roman Numerals will the letters V I X make when looked at in a mirror?

7   See how good a detective you are. Follow the facts of this murder mystery closely:

A man who was living by himself in a house in an isolated rural district was discovered dead one morning by his friend who had been visiting him until ten o'clock on the previous evening. An investigation showed that he had died of a bullet wound and that another bullet, which had apparently missed him, had shattered the clock, the hands of which indicated two o'clock. It was definitely proved by the dead man's friend that the clock had been shot sometime after his departure from the murdered man's home. A known enemy of the dead man against whom there was strong evidence of guilt was acquitted when two reliable witnesses swore that he had been with them from midnight until noon of the next day at a spot 10 miles from the murdered man's home.

Question: What was the fallacy in acquitting the dead man's enemy?

8   I am the son of your father's sister. What relative am I of yours?

9   What one word means both
   I   a form of physical competition
   II   a large class of people distinguished by common characteristics?

'Brain Twister'

10 If a hen and a half lays an egg and a half in a day and a half, how many eggs will seven hens lay in six days?

TEST 6

Possible Score 120

1   In a book of 100 leaves, what leaf is page 49 on?

2   A headless man had a letter to write;
He who read it had lost his sight;
The dumb repeated it word for word;
And deaf was he who listened and heard.

3   When seen in a mirror, which of the following words printed in capital letters will look the same as when viewed directly?

MAN   TOOT   DEED

4   How many black squares are there on a checker board?

5   A man while coming out of the door of his house in the morning notices that the sun is just rising above the horizon on his left. On this day it will take the sun 10 hours before it sinks below the opposite horizon. Upon returning while he is unlocking the door, the sun is still on his left and a quarter of the way above the horizon. Approximately how long has he been gone?

6   There are three doors to a house and three men who wish to enter them. They all enter at the same time, and no two men enter the same door together. How many possible ways are there for them to enter the house?

7   What word meaning 'a short distance' means if read backwards (from right to left) 'beloved creatures'.

8   There is a monosyllable which, if you add to it a single letter, becomes a word of three syllables. What is it?

9   Imagine three horizontal lines an inch apart, one directly under another. Then imagine three vertical lines also an inch apart, each cutting all three of the horizontal lines.

Â Â How many squares of equal size do these lines form?

'Brain Twister'

10   Dr. Johnson once defined 'network' somewhat in this manner: 'A construction of filamentous reticulations with interstices between the inter-sections.' But the boy's definition is to be preferred: 'A lot of holes tied together by bits of string.' Now, can you say promptly what the following defines: 'A diminutive, argentic, truncated cone, convex on its summit and semi-perforated with symmetrical indentations.'

TEST 7

Possible Score 120

1   A man and wife had four married daughters, and each of these had four children. No one in the three generations had died. How many people were there in the family?

2   There were a group of boys on bicycles playing follow-the-leader. There were four boys in front of a boy, four boys behind a boy, and a boy in the middle. How many boys were there altogether?

3   If you were attempting to climb an icy hill, and if, after every time you had taken two steps forward, you slid back one step, how many steps forward would you have to take to reach a point five steps in advance of the starting-point?

4   How will the following sentence, attributed to Napoleon, read if you start with the last word and read all the letters and words backwards?

'Able was I ere I saw Elba.'

5   How could I say to you in one word that you had some refreshment between 9 and 11?

6   If a hen and a half lays an egg and a half in a day and a half, how many and a half who lay better by half will lay half a score and a half in a week and a half?

7   See if you can detect any mistakes in the following extract from a traveller's diary:

While travelling in South America recently, I was especially interested in the peoples of Chile, Peru, Brazil, and Colombia. I was delighted also to hear some of the stories about famous old explorers, such as DeSoto, who discovered the Mississippi, and Balboa, who discovered the Pacific, thereby carrying the Spanish flag to remote parts of this continent. The whole of South America is fascinating to me, but the five countries mentioned above appeal to me particularly.

8   Assume that the earth is a perfect sphere and that a band is stretched about the Equator so that it fits snugly. If 1 foot were added to the length of the band, this additional length would cause the band to stand off a certain distance from the surface of the earth at all points. Would this distance be:

   I   imperceptible

   II   a fraction of an inch

   III   about 2 inches

   IV   1 foot ?

9   In the following word eliminate the second letter
     and every alternate letter thereafter. What word do
     the remaining letters form:

GLEAMS

'Brain Twister'

10   The first part of the name of a certain make of
     automobile is suggested by a word meaning 'call';
     the second, by a word meaning 'insinuation'. What
     is the make of the car?

TEST 8

Possible Score 110

1   How do you pronounce 'cho pho use'?

2   Listen carefully to the following story:

At 5 a.m. on September 22, during the war, Private Jones had just been relieved as sentinel by his comrade. He became engaged in a conversation with his commander, Captain Smith. Just before he left after receiving some instructions, he remarked, 'Well, sir, last night I dreamed that we weren't going to win this war, and my dreams seem always to come true.'

'Nonsense', replied the Captain; 'we've got to win and we've got to believe that we shall win. For once you're wrong.'

The Captain, who was in a hurry to leave on his furlough, then dismissed the private. When he returned from his leave several days later, however, he had Private Jones court-martialled.

Why was Private Jones court-martialled?

3   What one word means both 'a means of conveyance' and 'a procession'?

4　Which of the following liquid measures represents the smallest volume?

2 GALLONS　　　9 QUARTS　　　17 PINTS

5　A watch indicates that the time is quarter of twelve. If the entire dial were moved around to the right a distance equivalent to five minutes, what time would the hands indicate?

6　The first two syllables of the name of one of the States of the United States is suggested by a girl's name. The third syllable is suggested by a word meaning 'debark'. What is the name of the State?

7　A starts from a given point and walks steadily at the rate of 3 miles per hour. B starts from the same point 2 hours afterwards and walks in the same direction at the rate of 6 miles per hour. In what elapsed time, after A starts, does B overtake him.

8　Rearrange the following letters so that they make the name of an article of furniture:

CHOCU

'Brain Twister'

9 Nine boys and three girls agreed to share equally their pocket money. Every boy gave an equal sum to every girl and every girl gave another equal sum to every boy. Every child then possessed exactly the same amount. What is the smallest possible amount they each then held?

STRESSES AND DISTRESSES

I		**II**	
Par—50%		*Par—60%*	
1	comparable	1	acclimate
2	penalize	2	sinecure
3	gratis	3	data
4	inquiry	4	eczema
5	scion	5	schism
6	cello	6	chasm
7	joust	7	quay
8	gondola	8	grimace
9	heinous	9	façade
10	oleomargarine	10	flaccid

III		**IV**	

III		**IV**	
Par—60%		*Par—50%*	
1	aviator	1	epitome
2	mischievous	2	precedence
3	impious	3	incognito
4	culinary	4	jugular
5	Pall Mall	5	zoology
6	orgy	6	gaol
7	bouquet	7	hoof
8	antipodes	8	apparatus
9	vaudeville	9	adult
10	sacrilegious	10	antipode

SPELLING BEE

The following words are correctly spelled. Try them out on your friends.

I

Par—80%

1 all right
2 fiery
3 benefited
4 fulfilled
5 zephyr
6 sergeant
7 athlete
8 isthmus
9 attendant
10 superintendent

II

Par—50%

1. embarrass
2. naphtha
3. paraffin
4. liquefy
5. preceding
6. seize
7. siege
8. heinous
9. Philippines
10. Filipino

III

Par—50%

1. harass
2. picnicking
3. vilify
4. supersede
5. diphtheria
6. parallel
7. soliloquy
8. weird
9. hemorrhage
10. sacrilegious

LET THE GENIUS TRY THIS GROUP:

IV

Par—30%

1	kaleidoscope	6	sassafras
2	liaison	7	connoisseur
3	reconnoitre	8	rhododendron
4	camouflage	9	hieroglyphics
5	xylophone	10	bourgeoisie

THESE ARE EASY BUT TRY THEIR PLURALS:

V

Par—70%

1	solo	6	thief
2	banjo	7	beef
3	crisis	8	reef
4	stimulus	9	soliloquy
5	grouse	10	cupful

JUGGLERS

1   Juggle the letters in each of these words to make another word:

        RING   CAME

        TERSE   SCOPES

        BORED

2   Juggle each of these into two others:

        HADES   RIME

        SLOW   SLIDE

        SALT

3   Juggle each of these into three others:

        SPAN   EMIT

        PARSES   SERVE

        LEAD

4   Now juggle each of these into four others:

        PEARS   STIME

        STEAM   RISEN

        STALE

BLUNDERS

Par—60%

1   (Don't) (Doesn't) he know you?

2   Everybody took (his) (their) seat(s).

3   Give it to (whoever) (whomever) wants it.

4   Measles often (has) (have) serious effects.

5   There (is) (are) a door and three windows.

6   Father asked Fred and (I) (me) to do the job.

7   He said that we seemed to be (them) (they).

8   (It's) (Its) a fine day.

9   What do you think of (his) (him) winning the race?

10 She is one of those girls who (are) (is) usually sad.

II

Par—70%

1   This is a (healthy) (healthful) climate.

2   He is (likely) (apt) to come soon.

3   He is (likely) (liable) to help us.

4   He was (hanged) (hung) for treason.

5   He came (quite) (rather) early.

6   Yesterday I (lay) (laid) on the sofa for three hours.

7   The weather (effected) (affected) his health.

8   Slander has ruined his (character) (reputation).

9   The (discovery) (invention) of electricity was important.

10 He has (less) (fewer) studies now than he had.

HOW INTELLIGENT ARE YOU?

If you really want to know if you have any intelligence, take these tests. Do it privately so that if your score is low, your wife won't know that her suspicions are verified. If, perchance, you score higher than 85%, we suggest that you tell your boss and touch him for a rise. He will undoubtedly be happily surprised to see signs of intelligence.

Score 5 points for each question correctly answered.

WRITTEN TEST 1

Possible Score 100

1   Not a few persons do not think it unnecessary not to be dishonest in their dealing with others.

Does this mean the same as saying that many persons think it necessary to be honest in their dealings with others?

(Write 'yes' or 'no' on your answer sheet.)

2   The hands of a clock which is set by Daylight Saving Time are in a position so as to form a straight line. If the minute hand is on the figure 1, what time will it be by Standard Time in three-quarters of an hour?

3   'The man is a fox.'

Which one of the adjectives listed below could best be substituted for 'a fox' so as to convey the same meaning?

WISE   HAIRY   GREEDY
QUICK   CUNNING

4   What one word means both
    I   mark of identification
    II   torch?

5   My father is the brother of your sister. What relative
    am I of yours?

        COUSIN   NEPHEW   SON
        UNCLE   SON-IN-LAW

6   Read the following statement:

    'The army stood like a stone wall.' Which one of the
    words listed below best shows the quality common
    to both 'army' and 'stone wall'?

        IMPENETRABILITY   COURAGE
        HARDNESS   PERMANENCY

7   If 117 is divisible by 3, write the number 3 on your
    answer sheet, unless 186 is divisible by 4, in which
    case write the number 5 on your answer sheet.

8   C is to 3 as F is to what number?

9   Read the following sentence:

    'The pilot steered the ship of state over the rough
    sea of public sentiment.'

    Which of the statements below corresponds most
    nearly in meaning?

    I   The captain managed his ship well in a terrible
         storm.

    II   The pilot guided the Prime Minister's yacht
         over a rough sea.

    III The Premier ran the government well in spite
         of adverse criticism.

10 In the following series, how many numbers above 10 and below 20 are even?

6   25   10   5   19   11   22   9   12
18   20   33   16   21   13   14   15

11 What county in the United Kingdom begins with 'R' and contains 7 letters?

12 Jack is three years younger than James. John is two years older than Jack. What is James's age in relation to John's?

1 YEAR YOUNGER   4 YEARS YOUNGER
1 YEAR OLDER   4 YEARS OLDER

13 A person is a good friend if:

I   He is true to you in time of need.

II   He lends you money.

III He tells you that you are a good fellow.

14 If 1 = a, 2 = b, 3 = c, etc., what word does the following number make?

25,138

15 By eliminating one letter in each of four words in the following sentence, a new sentence of an entirely different meaning will remain.

They heard meat was stewed.

Write on your answer sheet the new sentence.

16   If three men can build four boats in two days, at the same rate, how long will it take one man alone to build two boats?

17   By rearranging the letters in the word 'plea' make three new words.

18   What one word in the following passage destroys the trend of thought?

In preparing for an important fight, a boxer trains strictly. He must live regularly, eat carefully, and exercise strenuously. For weeks before an important battle he undergoes numerous privations and forgoes many pleasures. Nevertheless, if he is unsuccessful in his subsequent bout, he is disappointed because his training efforts have not brought him victory.

19   How many odd-numbered circles are there below that do not contain any of the letters that appear in the word 'anxious'?

20 In the circles below select the number from the largest circle containing an odd number and no letter which appears in the word 'beat' and add it to the number in the smallest circle which contains one of the letters in the word 'abacus'. What is the result?

WRITTEN TEST 2

Possible Score 100

1   A man shouts in the direction of a cliff which causes an echo that he hears 2 seconds later. If sound travels at the rate of 1,100 feet per second, how far away is the cliff?

2   Which two of the following words are composed of the same letters?

     AGATE   AGITATE   GATES

     STAGS   STAGE   GRATE

3   In the sentence below each dash represents an omitted letter. Write completely the words that contain dashes.

    M–r– –es and s–a–ps often breed – –s–uit– –s.

4   Jones earns more money than Smith. Doe's salary is less than Johnson's. Johnson earns more than Smith but less than Jones.

    Who gets the greatest salary?

5   If you had half as much money again in addition to what you have, you would have 5s. How much have you?

6   What British coin is the same size as the circle below?

7   Letting 1 = a, 2 = b, 3 = c, etc., write the number which denotes the word 'hedge'.

8   What word meaning 'light blows' means, when it is read backwards, 'gaiter'?

9   The sum of the digits of certain dates (years) in the twentieth century up to the present time equals 13. What dates are these?

10   Write the following on your answer sheet and, by inserting two periods and a question mark, make the meaning clear.

     That that is is that that is not is not is not that so

11   What three numbers in the following series are divisible by 2, 3, 4, 6 and 8?

     64 66 48 52 74 24 88 32 96 16

12   Rearrange the following words into a true statement.

     Persons all geniuses insane are.

13 The first syllable of the name of a place in the British Isles is suggested by a word meaning 'harbour'. The second syllable is suggested by a word meaning 'earth'. What is the name of the place?

14 In the following sentence one word obviously destroys the meaning. Write on your answer sheet the word which, if substituted for the one improperly used, would make the sentence logical.

Since he was an honest man almost all his life, he was once guilty of stealing.

15 There are two different numbers between 1 and 10 the sum of which added to their product equals 35. What are the numbers?

16 In the following sentence, if the second word means 'ascended', write the first word in the sentence on your answer sheet, unless the sixth word does not mean 'quickly', in which case write the fourth word in the sentence on your answer sheet.

He climbed the steep hill rapidly.

17 What one word means both
   I   a vehicle
   II   a platform?

18 How many different letters of the alphabet are used in the following sentence?

The quick brown fox jumps over the lazy dog.

19 Mark on your answer sheet the second highest number that you find on the figure below:

592	932	391	915
646	869	341	914
846	211	921	586
833	528	933	593

20 On the figure opposite locate number 914. Count
    three squares to the left and one square above.
    Take the last digit of the number in this square.
    Remember it. Now locate number 528. Count one
    square to the right and three squares above. Take
    the middle digit of this number. Remember it. Now
    locate number 593. Count two squares to the left
    and one square above. Take the first digit of this
    number. Multiply this digit by the sum of the other
    two which you have in your mind. Write the result
    on the answer sheet.

MORONS' MORGUE

THE HORSE RACE

There were three horses running in a race. Their names were Tally-ho, Sonny Boy, and Juanita. Their owners were Mr. Lewis, Mr. Bailey, and Mr. Smith, although not necessarily in that sequence.

Tally-ho unfortunately broke his ankle at the start of the race.

Mr. Smith owned a brown and white three-year old.

Sonny Boy had previous winnings of £20,000.

Mr. Bailey lost heavily although his horse almost won.

The horse that won was black.

This race was the first race that the horse owned by Mr. Lewis had run.

What was the name of the horse that won?

THE MARINERS

There are three ships, the *Albatross*, the *Americus*, and the *Hispaniola*, on the sea sailing for the ports of Liverpool, New York, and Cherbourg, but not necessarily in that order. They are commanded by Captains Brine, Tarr, and Salt.

A few months ago Captain Tarr was the guest of Captain Brine on the *Albatross*.

The *Hispaniola* hit a derelict on her last crossing and as a result, for seven weeks previous to the present trip, was in dry dock for repairs.

The *Albatross* has just passed the *Americus* in mid ocean and shipped a stowaway back by the *Americus*.

Mrs. Salt, who usually travels with her husband, was yesterday discharged from the hospital where she was treated for a week for a severe attack of ulcers of the stomach. This unfortunate condition victimized her while she was three days from land and necessitated her immediate removal to the hospital when the ship docked.

The Captain of the *Americus* is preparing a report for his owners, Cartright and Smith, Ltd., of Liverpool, which he will have to deliver to their offices as soon as the ship docks.

What ship does Captain Tarr command and to what port is it bound?

ANSWERS

TEST 1

1   Robin.

2   4 days.

3   12.

4   5 minutes past 4 o'clock.

5   Milk, because cream comes to the surface.

6   11 steps.

7   Duck.

8   14 Combinations:

    A florin and a sixpence.

    A florin and 2 threepenny pieces.

    2 shillings and a sixpence.

    2 shillings and 2 threepenny pieces.

    1 shilling, 1 sixpence and 4 threepenny pieces.

    1 shilling, 2 sixpences and 2 threepenny pieces.

    1 shilling, 3 sixpences.

    1 shilling and 6 threepenny pieces.

    5 sixpences.

    1 sixpence and 8 threepenny pieces.

2 sixpences and 6 threepenny pieces.

3 sixpences and 4 threepenny pieces.

4 sixpences and 2 threepenny pieces.

10 threepenny pieces.

9   No one could possibly know of what the aviator was thinking because his death occurred before he could have told any one of his thoughts.

10   7 oranges.

TEST 2

1   2 days.

2   9/10.

3   Right.

4   Sunday.

5   87,310.

6   The fallacy is that Mr. Drake, who must have been looking out of the window on the right side of his car to see any possible damage, could not have seen the sun on that side while he was travelling north.

7   Threepence.

8   Hustle.

TEST 3

1 Sloop.

2 6 combinations: 123 213 312 132 231 321.

3 Sunday.

4 3 $1/2$ yds.

5 I   Patrick Henry, not Thomas Jefferson, said,
      'Give me liberty or give me death.'

   II   In 1775 George III, not Charles II, was King of
        England.

   III The Declaration of Independence was signed in
        Philadelphia, not New York.

6 45 minutes.

7 5—B is the second letter in the alphabet and E is the
   fifth.

8 The same: pod.

9 Between 2.10 and 3 o'clock.

10 He fills up the 4-gallon measure and pours it into
   the 7-gallon measure. Then he refills the 4-gallon
   container and pours from it into the 7-gallon

container as much as the latter will hold, or 3 gallons. This operation leaves him with 1 gallon in the 4-gallon measure. He completely empties the 7-gallon container and pours the 1 gallon into it. Then he again fills the 4-gallon measure and empties it into the 7-gallon measure which gives him the desired 5 gallons.

OR

He fills up the 7-gallon measure and from that he fills the 4-gallon measure, leaving 3 gallons in the 7-gallon measure. Then he empties the 4-gallon measure and pours the 3 gallons from the 7-gallon container into the 4-gallon container. Next he fills again the 7-gallon measure and from it fills the 4-gallon container. He now has 6 gallons in the 7-gallon measure. Then he empties the 4-gallon measure and refills it from the 6 gallons in the 7-gallon container, leaving him 2 gallons in the 7-gallon measure. Again he empties the 4-gallon container and transfers the 2 gallons that are in the 7-gallon container to the 4-gallon measure. Filling up the 7-gallon container again, he transfers from it the 2 gallons necessary to fill the 4-gallon measure. This operation leaves him with the desired 5 gallons in the 7-gallon measure.

TEST 4

1. He entered the door which the man had left unlocked.

2. 65 minutes.

3. 9 3/4 inches.

4. The father is 30 years old.

5. Vale, veil.

6. Chide.

7. 19,619.

8. It is the same.

9. 3 days.

10. 1/4 inch. When standing on a bookshelf in proper order, volume 2 is at the right of volume 1, making page 1 of volume 1 separated from page 1000 of volume 2 only by the two covers.

TEST 5

1   A 2-inch pipe fills the tank more quickly than two 1-inch pipes. The area of the mouth of the 2-inch pipe is twice as great as the sum of the areas of the mouths of the two 1-inch pipes, as may be ascertained by applying the formula—area of a circle.

2   Civic.

3   Mr. Smith's boyhood friend was a woman named Catherine and the mother of the girl.

4   Each parent had 3 children when they married and 6 were born afterwards.

5   Lord Rosebery, Prime Minister from March 1894 to July 1895.

6   XIV—14.

7   The basis of the acquittal was that the clock that had been shot fixed the time of the murder at 2 a.m., at which time the acquitted man proved definitely that he was 10 miles from the scene of the murder. However, if the clock had stopped at 2 o'clock on a previous day and was not running when it was shot, it would not indicate the time of the murder.

Nor would it have fixed the time of the murder if the murderer had set it at 2 o'clock after shooting it. The deed could have been committed by the acquitted man between the hours of 10 and 12 o'clock when no investigation of his whereabouts was made.

8   Cousin.

9   Race.

10   28 eggs. The common mistake that is made is figuring that 1 hen lay 1 egg in 1 day and that the answer, therefore, is 42. Actually, each hen lays only 1 egg in a day and one-half, or two-thirds of an egg in a day.

TEST 6

1　The 25th leaf.

2　The letter 'O'.

3　Toot.

4　32 black squares.

5　Approximately 7½ hours.

6　In 6 different ways: The squares below represent the doors. The men are numbered 1, 2, and 3 respectively. They might enter the doors in any of the following combinations:

	□	□	□
1	1	2	3
2	1	3	2
3	2	1	3
4	2	3	1
5	3	1	2
6	3	2	1

7　Step.

8　Smile (monosyllable), S(i)mile (three syllables).

9　4 squares.

10　A silver thimble.

TEST 7

1   26 people.

2   5 boys.

3   8 steps.

4   'Able was I ere I saw Elba.'

5   At-ten-u-ate.

6   The answer is half a hen and a half hen; that is, 1 hen. If 1½ hens lay 1½ eggs in 1½ days, 1 hen will lay 1 egg in 1½ days. And a hen who lays better by half, will lay 1½ eggs in 1½ days, or 1 egg per day. So she will lay 10½ (half a score and a half) in 10½ days (a week and a half).

7   There is only one mistake in the extract. He has named four countries and later referred to them as five.

8   The band would be almost 2 inches (1.91 inches) away from the earth at all points.

     This at first seems inconceivable and is not clear until one realizes that the radius of any circles, *regardless of its size*, must increase 1.91 inches if 12 inches are added to the circumference. This may be proved geometrically by the application of the following formula: circumference equals twice the radius × 3.1416. For purposes of simplification, using 'C' for 'circumference', 'R' for 'radius' and '3' for '3.1416', we arrive at the following:

$$C = 2 \times R \times 3 \text{ or } R = \frac{C}{2 \times 3} \text{ or } R = \frac{C}{6}$$

Let us apply this formula to a small circle measuring 6 inches in circumference: $R = \frac{6}{6}$ or the radius = 1 inch. Now let us increase the circumference by 12 inches or make it 18 inches.

$R = \frac{18}{6}$ or radius = 3 inches, which is a 2-inch increase. In the same manner let us find the radius of a circle 12 feet or 144 inches in circumference:

$R = \frac{144}{6}$ or radius = 24 inches. Now let us increase the circumference by 12 inches to 156 inches.

$R = \frac{156}{6}$ or radius = 26 inches, an increase of 2 inches. It is therefore apparent that the radius of any circle will increase approximately 2 inches when 12 inches are added to the circumference. The same is theoretically true of a band representing the circumference of the earth. A 12-inch increase in circumference would cause a 2-inch increase in radius. The 2-inch increase in radius would make the band stand out from the surface of the earth 2 inches at all points.

9   Gem.

10   Chrysler (Cry slur).

TEST 8

1   Chop-house.

2   The sentinel had been sleeping during his duty.

3   Train.

4   2 gallons.

5   20 minutes to 11 o'clock.

6   Maryland.

7   4 hours.

8   Couch.

9   Every boy at the start possessed 3d. and he gave ¼ d. to every girl; and every girl had 9d. of which she gave ¾ d. to every boy. Then every child would have 4½ d.

STRESSES AND DISTRESSES

I

	Word	*Usual Mispronunciation*	*Proper Pronumciation*
1	comparable	com par´a ble—accent on second syllable	com´ para ble—accent on second syllable
2	penalize	short 'e' as in pen	long 'e' as in 'feet'
3	gratis	short 'a' as in 'rat'	long 'a' as in 'grate'
4	inquiry	ĭn´ quĭ ry—accent on first syllable	ĭn´ quĭ ry—2nd 'i' long as in 'fine'—accent on 2nd syllable
5	scion	skeon	'c' not pronounced—sion—'i' as in 'fine'
6	cello	'c' as in 's'	'c' as in 'ch' in 'chin'
7	joust	'ou' as in 'out'	pronounced 'joost' in 'just'
8	gondola	gŏn dō´ la—accent on 2nd syllable	gŏn´ dŏ la—accent on 1st syllable
9	heinous	'ei' pronounced as 'i' in 'fine'	'ei' pronounced as 'a' in 'hay'
10	oleo-margarine	soft 'g' as in 'gym'	hard 'g' as in 'Margaret'

II

	Word	*Usual Mispronunciation*	*Proper Pronumciation*
1	acclimate	ăc´ clĭ māte—accent on 1st syllable	ăc´ clī măte—accent on 2nd syllable—'i' as in 'fine'
2	sinecure	'i' short as in 'sin'	'i' long as in 'fine'
3	data	first 'a' short as in 'rat'	first 'a' long as in 'date'
4	eczema	ĕk zē´ ma—accent on 2nd syllable and long second 'e'	ĕk zĕ´ ma—accent on 1st syllable and short 'e' in 2nd syllable
5	schism	'sch' pronounced as 'sk' or 'sh'	'sch' pronounced as 's'—sism
6	chasm	'ch' as in 'chew'	kăsm
7	quay	kwāy	kēy
8	grimace	grĭm´ ĭs	gri māce´ 'a' as in 'face'—accent on last syllable
9	façade	'c' as 'k'—2nd 'a' long as in 'made'	'c' as 's'—snd 'a' is broad as in 'ah'
10	flaccid	'cc' as 'ss'— flăs sĭd	first 'c' as 'k' —2nd 'c' as 's'— flak´ sĭd

III

	Word	*Usual Mispronunciation*	*Proper Pronunciation*
1	aviator	1st 'a' short as in 'have'	1st 'a' long as in 'gave'
2	mischievous	mĭs chēēv´ ius— extra syllable and accent on 2nd syllable	mĭs´ chĕv ous— accent on 1st syllable
3	impious	ĭm pī´ ous, accent on 2nd syllable, 2nd 'i' long as in 'pine'	ĭm´ pĭ ous, accent on 1st syllable, 2nd 'i' short as in 'pig'
4	culinary	'u' short as in 'cull'	'u' long as in 'cupid'
5	Pall Mall	paul maul	pĕll as in 'pelt'; mĕll as in 'melt'
6	orgy	hard 'g' as in 'get'	soft 'g' as in 'gym'
7	bouquet	'ou' as 'o' — bō-kāy	'ou' as 'oo' — bōōkāy
8	antipodes	silent 'e'; accent on 1st syllable — an´ tĭ podes	pronounce 'e' long as in 'me'—accent on 2nd syllable— an tĭp o dēēs
9	vaudeville	'au' as 'awe'; 1st 'e' pronounced—vau dah vil	'au' as 'o' in 'vōcal'; 1st 'e' not pronounced— vōd´ vĭl
10	sacrilegious	săc´ rē lĭ gius	săc´ rĭ lē gius, 'e' long as in 'be'

75

IV

	Word	*Usual Mispronunciation*	*Proper Pronumciation*
1	epitome	accent on 1st syllable —ĕ′ pĭ tōme and silent 'e' in last syllable	accent on 2nd syllable; last 'e' pronounced long as 'me'—ĕ pit′ ō mē
2	precedence	accent on 1st syllable; 2nd 'e' short as in 'end'— prĕ′ cĕ dĕns	accent on 2nd syllable; 2nd 'e' long as 'eke'— prē cē′ dĕns
3	incognito	accent on 3rd syllable; 2nd 'i' as 'ee'—in cŏg nēē′ tō	accent on 2nd syllable; 2nd 'i' short as in 'nip'— ĭn cŏg′ nĭ tō
4	jugular	first 'u' as in 'jug'	first 'u' as in 'oo'
5	zoology	first 'o' as 'oo'	first 'o' long as in 'go'—zō ol′ o ji
6	gaol	gōle or gāle	jail
7	hoof	'oo' as in 'hook'	'oo' as in 'choose'
8	apparatus	3rd 'a' short as in 'rat'	3rd 'a' long as in 'rate'
9	adult	accent on first syllable—a′ dult	accent on 2nd syllable—ă dult′
10	antipode	'e' long as in 'mē'; accent on 2nd syllable— an tip′ ō dēē	silent 'e'; accent on 1st syllable— ăn′ tĭ pode

SPELLING BEE (PLURALS)

1 solos

2 banjos

3 crises

4 stimuli

5 grouse

6 thieves

7 beeves

8 reefs

9 soliloquies

10 cupfuls

JUGGLERS

1

ring: grin

terse: steer

bored: robed

came: mace

scopes: copses

2

Hades: heads, shade

slow: lows, owls

salt: slat, last

rime: emir, mire

slide: sidle, idles

3

spans: pans, snap, naps

parses: spares, spears, sparse

lead: dale, deal, lade

emit: mite, time, item

serve: verse, veers, sever

4

pears: parse, spear, pares, rapes, spare

steam: meats, mates, teams, tames

stale: least, tales, slate, teals, steal

stime: times, mites, items, smite

risen: resin, siren, rinse, reins

BLUNDERS

I		**II**	
1	Doesn't	1	healthful
2	his seat	2	likely
3	whoever	3	likely
4	has	4	hanged
5	are	5	rather
6	me	6	lay
7	they	7	affected
8	It's	8	reputation
9	his	9	discovery
10	are	10	fewer

WRITTEN TEST 1

1   Yes.

2   6.50;   10 minutes to 7 o'clock.

3   Cunning.

4   Brand.

5   Nephew.

6   Impenetrability.

7   3.

8   6.

9   The Premier ran the government well in spite of adverse criticism.

10   Four.

11   Renfrew.

12   One year older.

13   He is true to you in time of need.

14   Beach.

15 The hard mat was sewed.

16 Three days.

17 Leap, peal, pale.

18 Nevertheless.

19 2.

20 7.

WRITTEN TEST 2

1   1,100 feet.

2   Gates, stage.

3   Marshes, swamps, mosquitoes.

4   Jones.

5   3s. 4d.

6   A Sixpence.

7   85,475.

8   Taps.

9   1903, 1912, 1921, 1930.

10 That that is is. That that is not is not. Is not that so?

11 48, 24, 96.

12 All insane geniuses are persons.
    (Or) Insane geniuses are all persons.
    (Or) Insane geniuses all are persons.

13 Portland.

14 Though or although.

15 3 and 8.

16 He.

17 Stage.

18 26.

19 932.

20 22.

THE HORSE RACE

Mr. Smith's horse could not have won, because the horse that won was black.

Mr. Bailey's horse did not win.

Therefore, Mr. Lewis's horse must have won.

Tally-ho could not have won, and so could not have been Mr. Lewis's horse, because he broke his ankle at the start; and Sonny Boy could not have been Mr. Lewis's horse because he had previously run.

Therefore, Juanita must have been Mr. Lewis's horse, the winner.

THE MARINERS

Brine is Captain of the *Albatross* because he was host to Tarr on that ship.

It is obvious from the statement about Mrs. Salt that her husband's ship has not been in dry dock just previous to this trip because she was taken off of it, ill, eight days ago when it landed.

Therefore, Salt's ship cannot be the *Hispaniola*, which has been in dry dock for seven weeks, and must be the *Americus*.

Tarr's ship then is the *Hispaniola*.

The last statement of the problem shows that the *Americus* is headed for Liverpool.

The *Albatross* must have New York for its destination because the fact that it shipped a stowaway back by the *Americus* proves that it was going in the opposite direction to the *Americus*.

Therefore, the *Hispaniola* must be bound for Cherbourg.

How to Live Like a Lord without Really Trying
Shepherd Mead

Do not fear being poor in England. In America the
upper classes are the people who have the money.
In England the upper classes are the people whose
ancestors made money long ago—long enough so that
everyone has forgotten how. It doesn't even matter very
much whether they have it any more. Some of the Best
People are as poor as they can be. No one will mind if
you have to be poor along with them. You, too, can live
the aristocratic life without spending any money. You
will just have to learn a few simple, but lordly skills...

ISBN: 978 1 85124 279 5

Hardback, £12.99
US$25.00

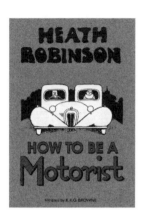

Heath Robinson: How to be a Motorist
W. Heath Robinson and K.R.G. Brown

This handy, decorative, valuable and uncostly volume
will appeal to everybody who is ever likely to drive, be
driven in, or get run over by a mechanically propelled
vehicle.

ISBN: 978 1 85124 434 8

Hardback, £9.99
US$17.50

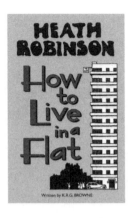

Heath Robinson: How to Live in a Flat
W. Heath Robinson and K.R.G. Browne

Once recovered from his initial bout of claustrophobia, the tenant of a modern flat should find it easy to readjust his life with the help of the hints set forth within this book. (The said hints can also be cut out, mounted on stiff parchment, and used as a novelty lamp-shade – if there is room in the flat for a lampshade).

ISBN: 978 1 85124 435 5

Hardback, £9.99
US$17.50

Secrets in a Dead Fish
The Spying Game in the First World War
Melanie King

Drawing on the words of many of the spies themselves,
this is a fascinating compendium of clever and original
ruses that casts new light into the murky world of
espionage during the First World War.

ISBN: 978 1 85124 260 3

Hardback, £8.99
US$15.00